RUSSIAN PROVERBS

Chris Skillen

Illustrations by VLADIMIR LUBAROV
In Association with TEXT Publishers, Moscow

Appletree Press

First published in 1994 by
The Appletree Press Ltd,
19–21 Alfred Street, Belfast BT2 8DL
Tel: +44 232 243074 Fax: +44 232 246756

Russian Proverbs

A catalogue record for this book is available from The British Library.

ISBN 0-86281-450-2

9 8 7 6 5 4 3 2 1

Introduction

Proverbs and traditional sayings are a link between the present and the past. Their imagery draws upon ways and lifestyles that have been eroded by industrialisation and urban life. Yet they do not lose their potency because what matters is not the precise form of words, but the irony or wisdom captured when the phrase was first coined. Every proverb has at least two levels. There is, first, the literal sense of the words and second, their irony, or wisdom. But this literal meaning is almost never the more important. The power of the proverb lies in the taking of its irony and wisdom from the past and applying it to a contemporary situation, where the logic of the literal is allowed to play on another, apparently different, situation.

The interplay between literal and hidden meanings has been particularly important in Russia. Over the course of this century, Russia's transition to a modern industrial society has been traumatic, not least because it has been accompanied by the ruthless suppression of dissent. In less difficult times, when it was possible to express discontent in private, among close friends, Russia's treasury of proverbs proved suitably oblique and indirect as a vehicle for people's true feelings about their world. And so these proverbs from Russia's distant past have continued to have relevance, not in spite of social change, but because of it.

◆

Не плюй в колодец – пригодится воды напиться.

Don't spit in the well, later you'll want to drink.

Не в свои сани не садись.

Don't drive in a sledge if it's not yours.

◆

На чужой каравай рот не разевай.

Don't open wide your mouth at the loaf of your neighbour.

Пьяному море по колено.

A drunk man thinks that the sea is knee-deep.

◆

В тихом омуте черти водятся.

Devils lurk in quiet pools.

◆

Гора родила мышь.

Sometimes the mountain brings forth a mouse.

◆

Один с сошкой, семеро с ложкой.

One with a plough, seven with a spoon.

◆

Рыбак рыбака видит издалека.

One fisherman spots another from afar.

Лбом стену не прошибёшь

You can't break through the wall with your forehead.

◆

Портной без штанов, сапожник без сапог.

**A tailor lacks trousers,
a shoe-maker lacks shoes.**

Не руби сук, на котором сидишь.

Don't cut the bough you are sitting on.

◆

Пристал как банный лист.

Sticks like a bath leaf.

◆

Решетом воду не носят.

You can't carry water in a sieve.

◆

Простота хуже воровства.

Naivety can do more harm than thievery.

◆

Старый друг лучше новых двух.

One old friend is better than two new ones.

Ночная кукушка дневную перекукует.

One cuckoo singing by night makes more noise than all the ones singing by day.

Нос вытащит – хвост увязит,
Хвостё вытащит – нос увязит.

Pity the man who pulls his nose out of the muck only to find his tail is stuck, and rescues his tail, only to find his nose in the muck.

◆

Что имеем, не храним,
Потерявши, плачем.

What we have, we lose,
when we lose, we weep.

◆

Стыд не дым, глаза не выест.

It is easier to bear shame than smoke in the eyes.

Куй железо, пока горячо.

Strike while the iron is hot.

Рыба с головы гниёт.

A fish begins to stink at the head.

◆

Соловья баснями не кормят.

Even nightingales can't live on fairy tales.

◆

Хлеб-соль вместе, а табачок врозь.

Bread and salt may be shared, but tobacco is best kept private.

◆

Лес рубят – щепки летят.

You can't chop down a forest without splinters flying.

◆

В Тулу со своим самоваром не ездят.

There's no point in taking your samovar to Tula.

Хорошо знает кошка, чьё мясо съела.

A cat always knows whose meat it eats.

◆

Русские волка ноги кормят.

Russian wolves live by their legs.

◆

Худой мир лучше доброй ссоры.

Better a bad peace than a good row.

◆

Правда хорошо, а счастье лучше.

It is good to know the truth, but better to be happy.

◆

С волками жить – по-волчьи выть.

Those who live amongst wolves must learn to howl like wolves.

◆

Что у трезвого на уме, то у пьяного на языке.

**What is on a sober man's mind
is on a drunk man's tongue.**

Не красна изба углами, а красна пирогами.

Do not judge a house by its appearance but by the warmth of the welcome.

Свои собаки грызутся, чужая не приставай.

It is a brave or foolish dog which joins a fight between friends.

◆

За двумя зайцами погонишься, ни одного не поймаешь.

Chase two hares and you'll catch neither.

◆

С милым рай и в шалаше.

**Where there is love,
even a hut will seem like heaven.**

Посади свинью за стол, она и ноги на стол.

Allow a pig to sit at your table, and it will put its feet on it.

◆

Волков боятся – в лес не ходить.

He who fears wolves will never go to the woods.

◆

Любишь кататься, люби и саночки возить.

Those who enjoy skiing downhill had better enjoy climbing uphill.

◆

Были бы кости, а мясо нарастёт.

If the bones remain, the flesh will come again.

◆

Ворон ворону глаз не выклюет.

One raven does not pick the eyes of another.

Яйца курицу не учат.

The egg shouldn't try to teach the hen.

◆

Не рой другому яму, сам в неё попадёшь.

**Don't dig a hole for somebody else,
lest you fall in it yourself.**

Каков поп, таков и приход.

Like priest, like flock.

Старого воробья на мякине не проведёшь.

**You can't catch an old bird
by offering it chaff.**

◆

Старая любовь не ржавеет.

Old love does not rust.

Чтобы узнать человека, надо с ним пуд соли съесть.

You never know a man until you've eaten a whole sack of salt together.

Кошке игрушки, а мышке слёзки.

The cat's playthings are the mouse's tears.

◆

Бодливой корове Бог рог не даёт.

God sends short horns to a cursed cow.

Кто не хочет кормить свою армию, тот будет кормить чужую.

He who will not feed his own army will feed another.

◆

Яблочко от яблоньки недалеко падает.

The apple never falls far from the apple tree.

◆

Под лежачий камень вода не течёт.

Water doesn't flow under settled stones.

◆

В чужих руках ломоть велик.

A morsel looks big in other people's hands.

◆

За одного битого двух небитых дают.

One man who's been flogged is worth two who haven't.

Бумага всё терпит.

Paper will accept any writing.

◆

У семи нянек дитя без глаза.

Give a child seven nannies, and it is sure to be neglected.

◆

Снявши голову, по волосам не плачут.

It's too late to worry about your hair when you are about to lose your head.